D0409579

LONDON BORO

What if we do nOthing?

# WASTE DISPOSAL

Christiane Dorion

FRANKLIN WATTS
LONDON•SYDNEY

First published in 2007 by
Franklin Watts
338 Euston Road
London NW1 3BH

Franklin Watts Australia
Hachette Children's Books
Level 17/207 Kent St, Sydney, NSW 2000

Produced by Arcturus Publishing Limited,
26/27 Bickels Yard, 151–153 Bermondsey Street, London SE1 3HA

© 2007 Arcturus Publishing Limited

Series concept: Alex Woolf
Editor: Nicola Barber
Designer: Peta Phipps
Consultant: Rob Bowden

Picture Credits
Corbis: cover bottom inset (Koopman), 5 (Ashley Cooper), 6 (Bob Sacha), 10 (Reuters),
16 (Jonathan Torgovnik), 18 (Dan Lamont), 21 (Vincent), 23 (Jean-Paul
Pelissier/Reuters), 24, 26 (H. David Seawell), 31 (Carlos Lopez-Barillas), 35 (Steve
Klaver/Star Ledger), 37 (Macduff Everton), 41 (Bernd Thissen/dpa), 43 (Christinne
Muschi/Reuters), 44 (Tony Kurdzuk/Star Ledger).
Corbis Sygma: 33 (Collart Herve).
EASI-Images: 29 (Rob Bowden).
Rex Features: cover background (Yan Morvan), cover top inset, 9 (Duncan Ridgley),
13 (Ray Roberts), 15 (Luigi Narici), 38 (Garo/Phanie).

Cover pictures: (background) e-waste on a landfill site; (top inset) man at a bottle
recycling depot; (bottom inset) recycling bin and logo.

Every attempt has been made to clear copyright. Should there be any inadvertent
omission, please apply to the publisher for rectification.

A CIP catalogue record for this book is available from the British Library

Dewey Decimal Classification Number: 363.72'8

ISBN: 978 0 7496 6967 6

Printed in China

| BARNET LIBRARIES | |
| --- | --- |
| | |
| 01-Oct-07 | PETERS |
| CNF | |
| | |

# Contents

# CHAPTER 1

# Choking on Waste

**It is 2025** and the country is facing a major crisis. The amount of waste produced every year is increasing rapidly. Landfill sites are full and incinerators are operating beyond their capacity. Waste is piling up in the streets and rubbish collectors are threatening to go on strike. The government is preparing for outbreaks of disease caused by the litter lying around and by contaminated water. Rats skittering through heaps of rubbish are now a common sight in the cities.

At the end of the 20th century, environmentalists urged governments to take action to reduce waste and to consider the impact on people's health and the environment. The response was to double the number of incinerators and to find new sites for landfills. More recently, officials gave the green light to relocate a village to create more space for waste. The first waste refugees of our time! While scientists are looking into ways of sending waste into space or burying it in the seabed, too many people carry on throwing away valuable resources and filling their bins every day.

### Too much stuff, too much waste

This scenario has not happened yet, but the disposal of waste has become a serious issue in many countries around the world. How did we end up in this mess? All animals create waste. In nature, what is waste for one species is food or a resource for another. For example, earthworms feed on dead plants, vultures eat animal carcasses and dead animals decompose, helping to create rich, fertile soil. Our early nomadic ancestors produced very little waste. Most of their waste, such as food, wood, bones and ash from fires, was biodegradable. This means that it was broken down naturally, with the help of micro-organisms such as fungi or bacteria, to become part of the earth again. The transition from nomadic hunter-gatherers to farmers meant that waste

## HOW MUCH WASTE DO WE PRODUCE?

In 2000, the world's people produced 12.6 billion tonnes of waste, more than 2 tonnes for every one of us; by 2050, we will produce a projected 26.7 billion tonnes each year, nearly 3 tonnes per person.

*Source: Tunza, UNEP magazine for youth*

was no longer left behind and methods of waste disposal had to be created. Archaeologists have discovered the world's first municipal landfill in Athens, created in 2500 BC.

The problem is that we are now producing more waste than can be absorbed by our natural environment, and an increasing amount of our waste is non-biodegradable. Since the start of the Industrial Revolution in the 18th century, and the development of factory machines, we have learned to produce large quantities of artificial materials such as nylon and plastic. With the development of new technologies, we have seen the invention of products such as microwave ovens, powerful cars, digital televisions, computers and mobile phones. Many of these products will take thousands of years to break down – and some have parts that will probably never fully break down. So the piles of rubbish keep growing.

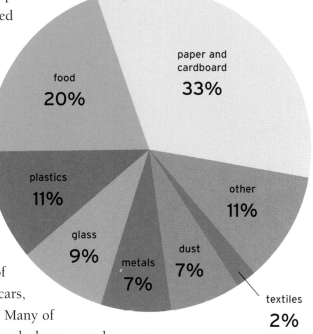

**This is what an average household dustbin in the UK contains. More than half of the contents could be recycled or composted.**

*Source: Waste Watch*

**This beautiful beach in Majorca, Spain, is covered in litter that has been washed up by the tide. Litter is a common sight everywhere around the planet. Materials such as plastic and metals, which do not break down easily, can be carried long distances by ocean currents and winds, ending up far away from the source of production.**

## All kinds of waste

Waste can take many different forms. It can be solid and visible, such as the contents of your bin or the local municipal dump. It can be liquid, for example water contaminated by chemicals used in a paper factory. Waste can also be gas, such as the emissions from cars and power stations. Most governments classify waste as 'municipal' and 'industrial'. Municipal solid waste, less than 10 percent of the waste produced in industrial countries, is the rubbish collected by local authorities from our homes, schools, offices, shops, restaurants and

Chemicals from industry and agriculture get washed into ponds, rivers and lakes, killing fish and other aquatic life. This lake in Kunming in China has turned green as a result of such pollution.

hospitals. Industrial waste, the main source of waste, comes from mining and quarrying, energy production, factories, construction and agriculture. It is estimated that for every tonne of waste we create when we throw stuff away, another 5 tonnes is created at the manufacturing stage and 20 tonnes where raw materials are extracted. For example, just to produce a Playstation, a rare metal called tantalum used in circuit boards needs to be extracted from the mountains of the Democratic Republic of Congo, leaving behind tonnes of mud sludge and large amounts of the chemicals used to separate the metal from its ore.

## What happens to our waste?

What happens if you throw an empty can of fizzy drink into the bin? If you live in the UK, the United States or Australia, it will probably be picked up by a truck and driven kilometres away to a landfill site, where it will gradually sink into the ground. If you live in Japan or Denmark, it will probably end up being burned in an incinerator.

### HOW LONG TO BREAK DOWN?

These are estimates of how long it will take for different items to decompose. The times vary depending on conditions such as amounts of sunlight or rainwater.

| Material | Example of decomposition time |
| --- | --- |
| Cans | 80 to 100 years |
| Cardboard | Several months to 5 years |
| Cigarettes | 12 to 40 years |
| Disposable nappies | 100 years to never |
| Fruit and vegetables | 6 months to 2 years |
| Glass bottles and jars | Never |
| Paper | 5 months to 50 years |
| Plastic bottles | 50 to 100 years, to never |
| Motor oil | 10 to 30 years |

Source: UK Composting Association and Waste Watch

## A trip to the landfill site

Dumping waste in landfill sites has traditionally been the easiest and cheapest option for most industrialized countries. A landfill is a designed structure built into or on top of the ground where rubbish trucks dump their loads of waste. The rubbish is compacted and covered up with a layer of soil to reduce odours and vermin. Landfills are not designed to break down waste, merely to bury it. They are like giant storage containers that slow down degradation and protect the environment from contamination. So, every day, the landfill gets fuller as more rubbish is brought in. Eventually, it fills up, is covered with soil, and becomes a permanent feature of the landscape. Closed landfills have been turned into parks, parking lots, golf courses and even ski slopes. When a landfill is full, another method needs to be found to deal with the waste.

## TREATMENT OF MUNICIPAL SOLID WASTE (FIGURES 2000/2001)

| Country | Total (million tonnes per year) | Landfill | Incineration | Recycling | Other (compost etc.) |
|---|---|---|---|---|---|
| United States | 208 | 56% | 15% | 22% | 7% |
| Japan | 55 | 6% | 73% | 14% | 7% |
| Germany | 49 | 25% | 22% | 27% | 26% |
| UK | 35 | 80% | 7% | 12% | 1% |
| Switzerland | 4.7 | 6% | 47% | 33% | 14% |
| Denmark | 3.5 | 10% | 52% | 22% | 16% |

*Source: OECD, Environmental Data, 2004*

## Old landfills for sale

Until the 1970s, most landfills were crude rubbish dumps used for the disposal of both municipal and industrial wastes. Little thought was given to health and environmental concerns. In 1978, events at Love Canal on the edge of the Niagara Falls, in the United States, brought evidence that heavy metals, chemicals and oil can seep out of old dumping sites many years after they have been covered. This

The increasing amount of waste we throw away in industrialized countries means that landfill sites such as this one in the UK are quickly becoming full.

seepage is known as leachate. From 1920 to 1953, Love Canal was used to dump industrial waste. Then, the site was closed and the canal area covered with dirt and presumed safe. It was sold to build a housing estate and promoted as a dream community. Gradually, toxic chemicals and gases seeped out of the ground, contaminating land and water and causing severe health problems for the local residents. The whole community had to be relocated and the area cleaned up. This is just one of many serious cases of contamination that have brought public attention to the issue of waste.

## The problem with landfills

Landfills take up space. They also cause pollution. The breakdown of organic waste inside a landfill produces gases such as methane and carbon dioxide which contribute to global warming. In many countries, new rules require the collection of methane gas. At some landfills the gas is collected, treated and sold as a commercial fuel. At others it is burned to generate steam and electricity. Modern landfills are also built in a way that prevents leachate from escaping into the groundwater. Nevertheless, environmentalists argue that landfills are time-bombs, their contents slowly being released into the air we breathe and the water we drink.

### Up in smoke

In many countries, especially in places such as Japan where space is limited, a large proportion of waste is burned in incinerators. Incineration is a more expensive option for dealing with waste, but it takes up less space than landfills and is seen as a safer method. Different types of waste can be burned, such as tyres, plastics and chemical substances. But, like landfills, incinerators can cause health and environmental problems. The materials burned do not simply disappear. Burning waste pumps toxic ash and gases into the atmosphere. Modern incinerators can recover some of the heat generated in incinerators to produce hot water and electricity. Environmentalists argue, however, that incinerators are inefficient at generating energy, producing more carbon dioxide per unit of energy than an old-fashioned, coal-fired power station. When waste goes up in smoke, we are left with large quantities of toxic ash that still need

Toxic pollutants from the chemical industry are spreading to the most remote parts of the planet, such as the Arctic and deep oceans. On 12 August 1999, in the northern Arctic Sea, Greenpeace launched its 'Down to Zero Toxics' campaign with the aim of eliminating toxic substances.

to be disposed of somewhere. Every 100 tonnes of burned rubbish leaves behind one-third of its weight in ash.

## Dumping in rivers and seas

Despite being against international law, the dumping of toxic and industrial waste in rivers, lakes and oceans still takes place in many parts of the world. Stories of factories dumping their waste into rivers or shipping it out of territorial waters to be dumped at sea are often reported in the newspapers. The dumping of everyday waste produced on board ships and military vessels is also a serious issue. Pollution may be carried thousands of kilometres by currents and tides, and pollutants can build up in the bodies of fish and other marine animals. The Inuit, living in the Canadian Arctic, have been affected by eating fish and seals with high levels of toxins. These toxins have been passed through the food chain from industrial pollutants and pesticides that were originally discharged thousands of kilometres away.

## Space junk

Not only are we polluting our planet, but we are also increasingly producing waste in space. With the development of satellites for telecommunications, military purposes and astronomy, an increasing amount of debris from old rockets and satellites is orbiting the earth. When a satellite is put in space, the rockets used to put it into orbit are discarded. A collision with even a small fragment can damage a satellite, shuttle or space station. In 1996, the French military satellite *Cerise* became the first casualty of space junk, damaged by a collision with the debris of a rocket.

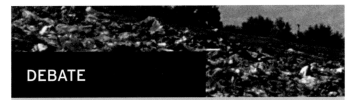

**DEBATE**

**You are in charge**

Following your government's proposal to build new incinerators, you are taking part in a regional meeting with other young people and representatives from government, industry, business and environmental groups to discuss the problem of waste. Some initial ideas have been proposed:

- The government needs to force change and make manufacturers responsible for the waste they produce.
- Local authorities need to make recycling easier for households, shops, schools, offices and hospitals.
- Individuals should be made to pay for the waste they produce.
- New technologies and methods of waste disposal should be explored, such as burying waste deep in the seabed.

Which options would you put forward to tackle the waste crisis?

# CHAPTER 2

# A Chemical Cocktail

**It is 2025.** An explosion of toxic waste in India has resulted in a catastrophic accident. This is the worst environmental disaster in history, with as yet unforeseeable consequences. Thousands of people have been killed or seriously injured, and the death toll is likely to rise dramatically over the next few years. Many of the country's rivers have been polluted by the accident and drinking water is now running short. Towns and villages have been evacuated and temporary shelters built.

For the past 40 years, environmentalists around the world have been urging their governments to legislate against the use of toxic chemicals. Yet industrialized countries have continued to produce increasing amounts of toxic waste. Despite international agreements, many countries have carried on exporting their waste illegally to places where regulations on toxic waste are non-existent. Forty country leaders, including representatives from some of the main polluting countries, are gathered today in Washington D.C. in the United States to draw up an action plan to eliminate the production of toxic waste and to ban international dumping.

## Toxic waste

Hundreds of millions of tonnes of toxic waste are produced and transported around the world every year, presenting a danger to people's health and to the environment. Waste is classified as toxic or hazardous if it is flammable, corrosive, explosive or contains poisonous substances. Most toxic waste comes from the production of chemicals and plastics, and about 90 percent is produced in industrialized countries. You are likely to find products with toxic components in your own home, such as batteries, computers, oil-based paint, cleaning products, pesticides and weed killers. However, the problem starts mainly when these products are broken apart or release their toxic ingredients into the

### MAKING A COMPUTER

The manufacture of one computer consumes 240 kg of fossil fuels, 22 kg of chemicals and 1,500 kg of water.

*Source: UN University, Tokyo*

environment. This is why such waste needs special handling for treatment, storage, transport and safe disposal. In recent years, as controls on waste disposal have tightened in many countries, companies have begun to export their toxic waste to countries which have better treatment facilities or less stringent regulations. In addition, products that are banned in many industrialized countries, such as asbestos and certain types of chemicals, are still exported to developing countries where they can be sold.

## E-waste

Since the 1980s, the high-tech boom has brought a new type of toxic waste from unwanted and unusable electronic and electrical equipment such as computers, televisions, VCRs, DVD players, game consoles, stereo equipment and mobile phones. Electronic waste, or 'e-waste', contains toxic components such as plastics and heavy metals which can release harmful toxins into the environment. Computers and electronic games are made of more than 1,000 different materials, some of which contain toxic components such as lead, mercury and cadmium.

The average computer has a lifespan of less than two years, and software companies constantly produce new programs that fuel the demand for more speed, memory and power. Today, it is often cheaper and easier to buy a new machine than to upgrade an old one. In 2002, the number of personal computers in the world reached 1 billion and sales continue to rise at a rate of around 130 million a year.

**The WEEE (Waste from Electrical and Electronic Equipment) man stands on London's South Bank in the UK. This sculpture, standing 7 m high, shows how many electrical and electronic goods are thrown away by the average person in the UK in a lifetime - over 3 tonnes.**

### WHAT'S IN A COMPUTER?

On average, a computer is made of:

| Material | Percentage |
|---|---|
| Ferrous metals | 32% |
| Plastic | 23% |
| Non-ferrous metals (lead, cadmium, antimony, beryllium, chromium and mercury) | 18% |
| Glass | 15% |
| Electronic boards (gold, palladium, silver, tantalum and platinum) | 12% |

*Source:* UNEP

Millions of mobile phones are produced each year, with a reduced lifespan, adding to the pile of high-tech junk. The cadmium from one mobile phone battery is enough to pollute around 600,000 litres of water – which is about a quarter of an Olympic swimming pool. Most of these high-tech products, when replaced, are simply dumped in landfill sites or burned in incinerators.

## Export of e-waste

When e-waste is recycled, strict health and safety regulations and high labour costs make the handling of its toxic components prohibitively expensive in many industrialized countries. As a result, many of these countries export their e-waste to countries with less stringent regulations and cheaper workforces, such as China, Pakistan and India. For example, the United States ships up to 80 percent of its recycled e-waste to Asia. Computers, printers, televisions and other e-waste sent for recycling are dismantled in large-scale yards, where thousands of people try to make a living by breaking up the electronic equipment and recovering valuable materials such as copper, steel, plastic and aluminium. Even schemes offering ways of reusing obsolete computers can be misleading. It is estimated that up to 75 percent of the computers and electronic goods shipped to Africa for reuse is actually junk which cannot be repaired or sold. Much of this equipment ends up in open dumps or burned, posing health threats to local populations.

## An e-waste village in China

Until recently, the Chinese village of Guiyu, in the southern province of Guangdong, had an economy based on rice cultivation. But, since 1995, it has become a booming e-waste village. While rice is still grown in the fields,

### THROW-AWAY PHONES

About 105 million phones are replaced every year in Europe. If you placed them one in front of another, they would form a line 14,700 km long, enough to reach from Cairo to Cape Town and back again! Standing on top of each other, they would be 342 times higher than Mount Everest.

*Source: www.weeeman.org*

### TYPE OF E-WASTE PRODUCED IN INDUSTRIALIZED COUNTRIES

| Type of e-waste | Percentage |
| --- | --- |
| Refrigerators | 20% |
| Information and communication equipment such as mobile phones | 15% |
| Electronic | 15% |
| Monitors | 10% |
| Televisions | 10% |
| Other electric appliances | 30% |

*Source: Basel Action Network, 2001*

all other available space is used for the recycling of e-waste. The average wage is about US$1.50 per day. Recycling involves dismantling electronic equipment and separating useful materials. Workers open toxic products such as computers and printer cartridges without any goggles, gloves or masks to protect them, as safety and protection of the environment are low priorities for their employers. Computer parts are burned to recover precious metals such as copper and gold, constantly filling the air with black ash. As a result, many people have developed respiratory and skin problems. Tonnes of toxic residues are dumped in surrounding fields, ponds and rivers. In 2000, water samples from a local river revealed lead levels 2,400 times higher than the recommended guidelines for drinking water. The villagers now import their water for drinking from a town 48 km away. Fishing ponds near the village are polluted. Guiyu is a real example of the impact of the e-waste trade.

**Many children in the village of Guiyu, China, work at dismantling electronic waste to help their families earn a living.**

## Responsible recyclers

Governmental and environmental organizations and industry are all developing initiatives to prevent the export of e-waste and to encourage recyclers to be more responsible. For example, in the United States the Rethink Initiative has been set up to help sellers find takers for their unwanted technological gadgets through the auction website eBay, and to offer solutions on how to recycle responsibly. The Silicon Valley Toxics Coalition has launched a campaign to pressure manufacturers to take full responsibility for their products. New computers with lead-free circuit boards and vegetable-based plastic components are coming on to the market. From 2004, the state of California introduced a fee on the sale of all new computer monitors and televisions to cover the cost of recycling. In Europe, the first e-waste recycling system was introduced in Switzerland in 1991, beginning with the collection of refrigerators and gradually including all other electric and electronic appliances.

In 2006, the European Union adopted the Waste from Electrical and Electronic Equipment (WEEE) directive, setting recycling goals for different appliances for its member countries and making producers responsible for the recycling of their electrical waste. Another European directive bans new electrical and electronic equipment that contains certain toxic substances, such as lead in computer circuit boards. Similar legislation requiring that sellers and manufacturers pay for the cost of recycling has been adopted in many Asian countries including Japan, South Korea and Taiwan.

## Ship-breaking

The ship-breaking industry is another major source of toxic waste. With the emergence of stricter environmental laws in industrialized countries, ship-breaking activities have moved to countries such as India, Bangladesh, Pakistan and China. About 50 percent of the ships salvaged in the world are recycled in Alang, a coastal town in India, while the second-largest ship-breaking operation is in the port of Chittagong, in Bangladesh. Large oil tankers, rusty car ferries and chemical carriers are brought on to the beach during high tide and, as the tide goes down, hundreds of workers dismantle the ships with blow torches and sledgehammers. They try to salvage what they can: steel, copper, useful machinery and furniture. However, many of

these vessels contain toxic materials and the coastal waters around these ports are heavily polluted with asbestos, heavy metals, oil and chemicals. Workers are paid about US$1.20 a day for this dangerous work in which they are exposed to extreme heat, toxic and flammable gases and dangerous chemicals – usually without any protective clothing.

**The Alang and Sosia ship-breaking yard in Gujurat, India, is the largest in the world, employing 35,000 migrant workers. The rate of accidents is very high due to gas leakage, explosions and lack of protective clothing.**

## Nuclear waste

Like all industries, the production of energy creates waste. Radioactive waste from nuclear power stations is highly toxic and has been generated for decades. Although it makes up less than 0.1 percent of the world's waste, it is a major source of concern. In a nuclear reactor, atoms of uranium are split to release energy. The irradiated fuel and old reactors are extremely dangerous and must be kept away from human contact, but some high-level radioactive waste will take over 20,000 years to decay. Since the invention of nuclear power in 1942, scientists have been looking for ways of getting rid of such waste, which is currently being stockpiled in specially designed containers.

## NUCLEAR FACTS

In 2004, radioactive waste was produced by 442 nuclear power plants, operating in 30 countries and supplying 16 percent of the world's electricity.

The vast majority of nuclear plants are in the United States, Canada and Western Europe.

The United States, with about 75 commercial nuclear sites, is expected to have 85,000 tonnes of spent fuel by the 2030s – well above current storage capacities.

Only temporary storage methods exist for the disposal of radioactive waste and none of the countries producing nuclear waste has so far managed to find a more permanent solution. Long-term storage deep underground is one possibility, but the problem is that the earth moves and no one can judge precisely where or when earthquakes will take place. The United States government has already approved a potential site for the disposal of nuclear waste at Yucca Mountain in the desert landscape of Nevada, about 150 km from Las Vegas. The proposed site will store all the high-level radioactive waste produced in the United States deep below the

The United States government hopes to store high-level radioactive waste in this underground tunnel inside Yucca Mountain, Nevada. Many people are strongly opposed to the project.

earth's surface in an underground tunnel. The plan is to transport waste by rail to Yucca Mountain by 2010. Like many nuclear facilities, the project is very controversial and many people are strongly opposed to it, especially local residents.

## A poisonous legacy

Serious accidents can happen with nuclear reactors, causing the release of high levels of radiation. In 1979, a reactor overheated at the Three Mile Island nuclear plant in Pennsylvania, in the United States. Although there were no casualties, it fuelled public concern over the safety of nuclear energy. In 1986, a blast ripped through the nuclear power plant of Chernobyl, in the former Soviet Union, killing more than 56 people and affecting the long-term health of thousands more. This was the worst accident in the history of nuclear power. A cloud of radioactive waste drifted over northern Europe and beyond. Today, many farms across the north of Europe are still contaminated by the Chernobyl fallout. Concern over nuclear safety was renewed in 2000 by a fire at a Japanese fuel reprocessing plant and, in 2005, by an undetected leak of radioactive materials at Sellafield power station in the UK.

## DEBATE

### You are in charge
You are delighted to get your new MP3 player after months of saving money for the latest and most powerful model. The question is, what will you do with your old model, your redundant CD player and your old sound system?

■ Give them to a charity shop.
■ Throw them in the bin, as they don't work very well.
■ Leave them in your drawer or the attic in case you need them one day.
■ Put them in a special recycling bin for electronic goods.

Which option would you choose? What will be the impact on people and the environment?

# CHAPTER 3

# Living in a Material World

**It is 2025.** Over the last 20 years, new laws have gradually been adopted in the United States and Europe to make producers pay for their waste. Manufacturers and businesses now have to cover the cost of handling the waste that they create. Due to successful campaigns run by consumer associations, some products have been withdrawn from the market because of their toxic content or excessive packaging. Manufacturers have been forced by governments to reduce the amount of packaging on other products, and to make use of compostable materials. Environmentalists are delighted. But the extra costs mean that many businesses are in danger of closing down. Other businesses are threatening to move their operations to places where environmental laws are less stringent, in order to try to remain competitive. Many jobs have already been lost, and the price of electronic products is set to increase by 15 percent in the next two years.

### A disposable planet?

As we aspire to improve our standards of living, we produce more waste. The mobile phone market is a good example of our 'throwaway' society. In the UK, people replace their mobile phones on average every 18 months, even though a phone could last for up to eight years. This means that about 15 million mobile phones are replaced each year, and many of the unwanted phones are simply thrown away. Disposable goods have become part of our lives, from toothbrushes to cameras, pens, plastic cups, tissues and batteries. In China, people throw away 90 billion disposable chopsticks every year, using more than 25 million trees and bamboo plants annually.

### History of packaging

More than half of what goes in our bin is packaging. Today almost everything we buy and produce is contained and heavily wrapped in different layers of materials such as paper, board, plastic, glass, steel and aluminium. Packaging really took off during the Industrial Revolution in Europe, when factories allowed mass production and trade began to flourish between countries. New technologies and materials were developed to preserve and transport food and products safely and efficiently around the world. The invention of fridges and microwave ovens resulted in the development of heavily packaged fast-food and convenience food, contributing to the mountain of waste. Through the Internet, we can now order books, furniture, electronic games and clothes from all around the world, safely delivered in packaging to our doorsteps within a few days. But at what cost to the planet?

## PACKAGING MATERIAL IN MUNICIPAL SOLID WASTE IN THE USA

| Material | Percentage of total weight |
|---|---|
| Paper/board | 52% |
| Plastics | 16% |
| Glass | 14% |
| Metals | 6% |
| Mixed materials | 12% |

*Source: USA Environmental Protection Agency, Facts and figures for 2003.*

### Drinks packaging

Think about what you drink every day. How many plastic bottles, cans and glass bottles do you use? While our early ancestors drank out of leather flasks or carved wooden vessels and used leaves for wrapping and storing their food, the invention of synthetic materials has enabled us to create different forms of packaging that are more hygienic and resistant to extreme temperatures. In 1944, a Swedish designer called Ruben Rausing created a new kind of milk container made of plastic-coated paperboard as an alternative to breakable glass. In 2003, Tetra Pak, the company founded by Rausing, produced 105 billion packages which are used around the globe to store and transport goods such as fruit juice and milk. Such packaging is essential for the modern food industry. In developing countries where packaging is often minimal, 30 to 50 percent of the food produced rots or goes off before it even reaches consumers.

Food packaging contributes to the mountain of waste we produce every day. In 2001, in the UK alone, households produced the equivalent weight of 245 jumbo jets per week in packaging waste.

The problem is that, increasingly, plastic containers and cartons form a major part of our municipal waste. In Western Europe, 61 percent of the total plastic waste comes from packaging. Because of public pressure and financial benefits, major companies are starting to reduce the weight and volume of their packaging and use materials that can be recycled or composted.

## A BRIEF HISTORY OF PACKAGING

| Timeline | Invention |
|---|---|
| Pre-1800 | Sacks, chests and barrels are used for transporting and storing bulk goods |
| 1800-50 | Individual cartons and cardboard boxes are introduced |
| 1840 | Airtight metal cans are widely used |
| 1852 | First machine for making paper bags is invented in United States |
| 1880s | Mass-production, folding cartons and colour-printing produce development of branded goods |
| 1892 | Metal tubes for toothpaste are introduced |
| 1894 | First Coca-Cola bottles |
| 1907 | First commercial plastic is invented |
| 1920s | Potato crisps are sold in tins to keep them fresh<br>Cellophane is used extensively for wrapping items such as sweets |
| 1923 | Birdseye makes first frozen foods, sealed in cartons and wax paper wrappers |
| 1933 | Polythene is invented by ICI, a UK chemicals company |
| 1940s | Aerosols become popular<br>Plastic is introduced as a packaging material |
| 1950s | Tetra Pak invents the aseptic milk carton<br>Polythene bags are widely used |
| 1970s | Many new plastics are developed for packaging, including the PET (plastic) bottle for carbonated drinks |
| 1980s | Growth of convenience-food packaging, including special designs for microwave ovens |
| 1990s | New plastics can be put in a hot oven for cooking food<br>New technologies in packaging help preserve food longer |

## Battle of the bag

Most households have a cupboard full of old plastic bags. Although these bags make up a small proportion of our waste, they have become a real problem for the environment. According to the non-governmental organization (NGO) Clean Up Australia, Australians use more than 6 billion plastic bags per year. If they were tied together, these bags would form a chain long enough to go around the world 37 times. Most of these bags end up in landfills, stuck on trees or floating in the ocean, and they can take up to 1,000 years to break down. Plastic bags pose a real danger for wildlife both in the marine environment and in the countryside. Tens of thousands of whales, birds, seals and turtles are killed every year as they often mistake plastic bags for food such as jellyfish.

Different countries have adopted a range of measures to discourage the use of plastic bags. For example, in Ireland and areas of Australia and China, shoppers have to buy their plastic bags instead of being given them free. In other countries, such as India and Bangladesh, a total ban on plastic bags has been implemented as in the past they have blocked drains in cities and worsened the effects of floods. The ban has lead to a revival in the jute bag industry. In South Africa, the government allows only the production of more durable plastic bags, hoping that the extra cost of these bags will push retailers and consumers to use fewer bags for longer.

Sheep graze in a field in southern France that has been covered with plastic bags blown by strong winds from a nearby waste dump. Plastic bags, whether thrown away deliberately or blown from open waste dumps, create many problems for wildlife and the environment. They end up blocking drains, trapping birds and killing animals.

## The hidden story of a product

Every day people buy or use compact disks (CDs) to listen to music or play games on their computers. But have you ever thought about how CDs are made, what materials are used, or what happens to them when you don't want them any more? Looking at the life cycle of a product such as a CD helps to understand the connections between the use of natural resources, energy, production of waste and wider environmental issues such as climate change. This means looking at the entire production system, from extracting and processing raw materials, to the product's final use when you buy the CD. Waste is created at each stage of the life cycle, and therefore solutions need to be found for each of these stages.

Choosing a CD in a music store. Making products such as CDs and DVDs consumes natural resources, produces waste and uses energy. Changes in the way we produce, use and dispose of products could make huge reductions in waste.

## Production of a CD

### 1. Extraction of raw materials

To make a CD, you need different materials such as aluminium, plastic, glass, gold, silver, nickel, chemicals and water. Each material has its own life cycle, involving the use of natural resources, energy and the creation of waste.

### 2. Processing

Materials extracted from the earth must be processed before manufacturers can use them. For example, bauxite is transformed into a substance called alumina, which is then turned into aluminium.

This process creates a highly toxic waste called 'red mud'. To make plastics, crude oil from the ground is combined with natural gases and chemicals in a manufacturing plant, generating toxic waste and emissions. Then all of these raw materials must be transported to the place where the CDs are to be manufactured.

### 3. Manufacturing

A machine creates the core of the disk, a millimetre-thick piece of plastic. The plastic is melted and put into a mould and tiny indentations with digital information are stamped. These will allow the CD player's laser to read the CD. The CD is then coated with layers of aluminium and plastic to protect against scratching and corrosion. Most CDs have a decorative label and the printing process involves the use of different materials such as stencils and ink.

### 4. Packaging

CDs are packaged in clear or coloured plastic cases or cardboard boxes and covered with plastic shrinkwrap. This packaging can be made from recycled or raw materials. But when broken or no longer used, CD cases often end up buried in the ground or burned in incinerators, producing toxic emissions.

### 5. Transportation

Once the CDs are packaged, they are ready to be sent to distribution centres and retailers. They are transported by truck, rail or plane, requiring the use of fossil fuels for energy and therefore producing greenhouse gases.

### 6. Disposal or recycling

If properly stored and handled, most CDs will last for decades or probably centuries – until a new technology makes them redundant! Then they will probably end up in a cupboard, buried in the ground or burned. The good news is that the use of MP3 players and Internet downloads is already reducing the waste created by the manufacturing of CDs.

---

**CD FACTS**

In the United States alone, more than 45 tonnes of CDs become obsolete or unwanted each month. More than 55 million boxes of software go to landfills and incinerators each year.

Several companies in Europe and in the United States now recycle old CDs and DVDs into high-quality plastic for reuse in products ranging from car parts to office equipment.

One recycling business in San Jose, California, processes a million CDs every month.

*Source:* Worldwatch Institute

## Closing the loop

The key for producers to reduce waste is to 'close the loop'. This means reusing materials in the manufacturing process and converting unwanted waste into useful resources wherever possible. 'Closing the loop' not only reduces waste but also helps to conserve resources and save energy.

**Beams and pipes made of recycled aluminium are ready for shipment in Virginia, United States.**

A good example is the town of Kalundborg in Denmark, which has developed a unique system of reusing waste. Factories, businesses and the municipality have worked closely together since the 1970s to use each other's waste materials and surplus energy. For example, the oil refinery supplies its treated waste water to the coal power station for use in its cooling process. In return, the power station supplies the refinery with steam for use in its refining process. The waste gases from the refinery are used as fuel for the power station, and for two nearby factories producing plasterboard and chemical substances. Steam from the power station provides heating to a local pharmaceutical company, whose sludge waste is used to make fertilizer.

## Clean production

Since the 1990s, the concept of clean production has been promoted by environmentalists, progressive business

### DEBATE

**You are in charge**
You work for a major mobile phone company and have been asked to look at creative ways of reducing packaging and waste. The following ideas are being discussed:

■ Invest money to research new forms of biodegradable packaging.
■ Provide incentives to increase the recycling of packaging materials.
■ Create mobile phones that last longer and encourage consumers to keep them for longer.
■ Make thinner and lighter packaging out of recycled materials.

What would be your priority? Can you think of any other ways of reducing packaging?

people and some government officials. Clean production is not just about making things in factories in a cleaner way to reduce toxic waste. It is a way of looking at the impact of design and consumption on the environment. Cleaner products are being designed to last longer and to be reused, with minimal use of energy, water and raw materials. For example, the US company Hewlett Packard has developed a safe cleaning method for computer chips using carbon dioxide instead of toxic solvents. In 1999, IBM introduced the first computer that used 100 percent recycled resin instead of plastic. Packaging is also being rethought, by using non-toxic and recyclable materials and by reducing the amount of materials used. In 2002, Nestlé UK changed the packaging of many of its products and saved 240 tonnes of metal and 208 tonnes of paper and board in one year.

# CHAPTER 4

# A Tale from the South

**It is 2025.** An old man is sitting with his grandchild on the veranda of his house, in Nairobi, Kenya. "When I was young," he says, "I lived with my mother and seven brothers and sisters on the edge of the city. I stopped school at 11 years old to help my mother on the dump. We had to sift through rubbish all day long, hoping to find something that could be reused or recycled. I used to cut myself all the time and I had to carry a heavy bag on my back. Next to the rubbish dump was a mountain of old tyres that nobody seemed to want. That's where the idea came to me. Today, I employ 100 people to make sandals, rubber boots and bags from recycled tyres. My company has formed cooperatives in five African countries, and our products are now bought everywhere in the world via the Internet. I've seen similar enterprises emerging in America and Europe where the dumping of old tyres has become a real problem. I go to conferences all over Africa to tell my story and to encourage other people to follow my example. One day, my child, all this will be yours. You will never have to pick other people's rubbish to earn a living as I once did."

### Less wealth, less waste

More than half of the world's municipal waste is produced in industrialized countries where only 16 percent of the population lives. On average, a person living in the industrial world consumes 19 times more aluminium, 14 times more paper, 13 times more iron and steel and 10 times more petrol than someone living in the poorer countries. It has been estimated that if the rest of the world consumed as much as people living in the industrialized countries, we would need the equivalent of four extra Earths! In countries with fast economic growth, such as China and India, consumption is increasing rapidly – as well as the amount of waste. In poorer countries in Africa, Asia and Latin America, where resources are limited, repairing, reusing and recycling remains common practice.

## WASTE MANAGEMENT

- Only between 25 and 55 percent of all waste produced in large cities is collected by municipal authorities.
- It is estimated that more than 5 million people die each year from diseases related to inadequate waste disposal systems.
- Approximately 3,500 tonnes of waste are produced every day in Dhaka, the capital of Bangladesh. Around 51 percent is collected and transported to open dumps, 26 percent ends up in backyards, 11 percent is left on roadsides and open spaces, 9 percent is recycled by waste pickers. Only 3 percent is recycled where it is generated.

*Sources:* United Nations; Dhaka City Corporation

**Waste is a useful resource in Uganda, where kitchen utensils and lanterns are made out of recycled materials.**

### Rubbish factories

Amadou lives on the outskirts of Dakar in Senegal. Like millions of people in Africa, he lives in a slum on the fringe of the city, between mountains of old tyres and an old woman's shop selling plastic containers and scrap metal. Like many, he has left the countryside to find employment and a better life in the city. His home is made of the materials he could find and reuse and he has no formal address. Where Amadou lives, there are no basic services such as running water, toilets or electricity. There are no rubbish collections, so the mountains of waste build up. People in the community dispose of their waste however they can. They burn flammables and the rest ends up in rivers, ditches or streets.

In Amadou's world, waste is a resource. Wood and metal scraps are useful materials for his home, and empty tins become water containers or drum toys for his children. All over the world, city dwellers generate two to three times more rubbish than their rural counterparts and many cities in developing countries have inadequate facilities for disposing of waste. Most of the waste ends up in the streets and in open spaces. Up to 95 percent of the waste that *is* collected is thrown into open dumps. But the city rubbish collectors do not come as far as Amadou's settlement.

## RUBBISH PICKERS

Up to 2 percent of the developing world's urban population survives by scavenging. Each day in Kolkata, India, 20,000 waste pickers scour every metre of the city's municipal dumps, sorting and collecting rubbish.

In Mexico City, rubbish pickers have a life expectancy of 39 years due to high rates of infection and disease, compared with 67 years for the general population.

*Source: Tunza* UNEP magazine for youth

### Living in other people's rubbish

Bantar Gebang is one of the largest rubbish dumps in Jakarta, the capital of Indonesia. The dump has been closed and reopened many times, as the city government tries to cope with the disposal of the city's rubbish. People who live near Bantar Gebang have long campaigned for its complete closure, but they are fiercely opposed by the rubbish pickers who make a living by sifting through the waste brought by rubbish trucks from all over the city. The rubbish pickers search for plastic, glass, metal and cotton. Their pickings are sorted and given to different 'dealers' for different materials. On the edge of the dump, the homes of the rubbish pickers are made from scrap wood, corrugated iron and any other materials they can find. A wooden shed with chicken wire for windows is used as a school. The children go to school in shifts – the rest of the time they help their parents on the dump. Diseases such as typhoid and tetanus are common and accidents are frequent.

## A global phenomenon

Rubbish pickers are a common sight in many developing countries, where large numbers of women, men and children collect, sort and sell waste from households, streets, factories, dumps and rivers in order to make a living. They play a vital role in the recycling chain but are often either ignored or forgotten. Living from other people's rubbish is also on the increase in the large cities of North America and Europe. With the rapid expansion of cities, lack of housing and increase in population, a growing number of people have ended up living on the street in extreme poverty. Many of them are children who have run away from home. Homeless people often recover materials that can be used as shoes, clothing and bedding. They also pick up cans and bottles that can be exchanged for money, and sometimes eat scraps of food from street bins or fast-food outlets.

**A man collects plastic items for recycling in an improvised shed on Guatemala City's main rubbish dump.**

### Getting organized

Cooperatives of rubbish pickers are emerging across Latin America and Asia. Once organized, groups can bargain better prices for the waste they collect and negotiate good contracts with municipalities, governments and businesses. In Colombia, a non-governmental organization called the Fundación Social helps rubbish pickers to form cooperatives and provides loans and advice to new organizations. One of these cooperatives is made up of 1,000 waste pickers, 60 percent of whom are women. They earn 1.5 times the minimum wage and qualify for loans, accident insurance, and scholarships to continue their studies. In the city of Pune, India, a cooperative of 5,000 waste pickers has been appointed to organize daily door-to-door collection of rubbish from houses and offices. And in Rio de Janeiro, Brazil, women have formed a cooperative to make use of their crochet and patchwork skills to transform old fabrics into clothes and household products such as lamps, rugs, pillows and sofa covers. Similar networks are developing in Argentina, Indonesia, Mexico and the Philippines.

In Cairo, Egypt, a community of waste collectors has created a unique waste collection system. Up to 3,000 tonnes of household waste are collected each day by waste collectors and recyclers known as *zabbaleen*. The *zabbaleen* originally came from the south of Egypt and migrated to the city to earn their living by turning municipal waste into resources. Without the help of government or outside agencies, they set up a door-to-door collection system, with each family working on its own daily route, to collect and separate household rubbish. Recyclable materials are resold at market rates, food scraps fed to pigs and the rest sent to landfill. Most of the *zabbaleen's* income comes from the sale of recyclable materials and 80 percent of the waste they collect is recycled. However, the *zabbaleen's* way of living is now threatened by government plans to contract a foreign multinational company to collect and landfill all of Cairo's waste.

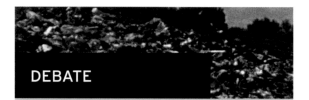

**DEBATE**

**You are in charge**
Think of the story you will tell your grandchildren in 60 years' time, about the day when the waste crisis reached its peak and the country came to a halt. The refuse collectors stopped collecting the rubbish because of protesters preventing them from getting to the incinerators and landfill sites. The government started to charge huge taxes to collect the rubbish from your home. Your family and neighbourhood had to find creative ways of reducing the amount of waste produced. What actions did you take on that day?

### A visionary mayor in Brazil

In Brazil, the mayor of Curitiba has set up with his citizens a unique system of waste disposal. Faced with full landfills and mountains of waste, he decided to borrow money to build a recycling plant for the city. Curitiba's citizens separate their rubbish into just two categories, organic and inorganic, which are picked up by two different kinds of trucks. A campaign in schools and neighbourhoods has encouraged people to recycle and separate their waste before collection. Poor families living in squatter settlements bring their rubbish bags to neighbourhood centres, where they exchange them for bus tickets, eggs, milk, vegetables and fruit. Schools are given notebooks and toys in return for their metal, glass and paper. The rubbish goes to a plant, built out of recycled materials, which hires unemployed people to separate bottles, plastic and cans. Two-thirds of the city's daily waste is processed at the plant. Recovered materials are sold to local industries. The recycling programmes cost no more than the old landfill, but the city is cleaner, jobs have been created, farmers are supported and poorer people get help with food and transportation.

**The inhabitants of the squatter settlements outside Curitiba, Brazil, are given food vouchers and bus tickets in return for their waste.**

# CHAPTER 5

# War on Waste

**It is 2025.** The Smith family are ten years into their Charter towards achieving Zero Waste. Zero Waste is the name given to a radical approach to minimize and recycle waste at home, school and work. It means using products for longer, recycling materials and composting organic waste. It also means reducing the pressure on the world's forests, soils and mineral resources. The Smith family has committed to incorporating the three 'R's into their daily routine – reduce, reuse and recycle. This has changed their lives. They walk and cycle, use public transport or, if they really need to, their electric-powered car. They compost organic waste and recycle cardboard, paper, fabric, plastic, glass and cans. They try to buy in bulk to reduce the amount of packaging. Most of their clothes are made from organic compostable cotton and recycled synthetic materials. They wear fashionable hemp and natural rubber shoes. The modern furniture in their house is toxin-free and made from recycled bottle tops and biocomposition, a material stronger than oak. Part of their pledge is to persuade at least ten of their friends and neighbours to commit to the Charter.

## Reducing waste

The best solution to the waste crisis is to reduce the amount of waste we create. Our daily choices determine the amount of waste we produce. Although our bins represent only a small part of the total waste generated, it is an important part. Changes in the way we buy, use and dispose of products could make huge reductions in waste. The first question to ask ourselves is whether we really need to buy a new product, or throw away an old one. Old computers, sound systems, books and clothes can be given to friends, family or charity shops, or sold in car boot sales or via the Internet. When we buy things, we can reduce waste by avoiding over-packaged goods or always taking our own shopping bags to reduce the use of disposable plastic bags. We can also make sure that we buy non-toxic, durable

and recyclable products, or products made of recycled materials. For example, buying printer cartridges that can be refilled reduces toxic waste.

## Sustainable consumption

As consumers, we have considerable power and we can make a real difference. By changing our shopping habits, we put pressure on businesses and industries to rethink the way they produce and package their products. Sustainable consumption is about using goods and services that meet our basic needs and bring a better quality of life for all, whilst minimizing the use of natural resources, waste and pollution. It is also about sharing resources between rich and poor and acting with concern for future generations.

A boy recycles a bottle at his school in the United States. We produce and use 20 times more plastic today than we did 50 years ago. Recycling of plastic is becoming more popular, transforming old bottles into new everyday items such as fleeces, CD cases or filling for sleeping bags.

## FANTASTIC PLASTIC?

Plastic is one of the most commonly used materials today as it is light and strong, and does not break easily. But did you know that:

- It takes one full cup of crude oil to make the plastic for each disposable nappy.
- Toothbrushes represent over 45 million kg of plastic waste each year.
- Recycling a single plastic bottle can conserve enough energy to light a 60W light bulb for up to six hours.
- Recycling plastic saves between 65 percent and 80 percent of the energy required to make new plastic and two-thirds of the sulphur dioxide emissions.
- It takes about 25 recycled plastic bottles to make one fleece jacket.

Source: www.zerowaste.co.nz

## A different destination

If we can't reduce or reuse, then recycling is a good option. Let's rewind and go back to that can of fizzy drink you threw in the bin (see page 7). What would happen if you had put it in the recycling box instead? It would have been picked up by a recycling truck and dropped at a centre where cans, glass, paper and plastic are sorted. Then it would have been squashed with other cans into big bales and taken by another truck kilometres away to the aluminium can factory. At the factory, the bales would have been shredded into small pieces, cleaned, melted down and rolled like pastry into thin sheets. New cans for fizzy drinks would then be produced.

But did you forget to put your can in the recycling box? That's what happens to 80 million food and drinks cans every day in the UK. Like everything else that is bundled into bin bags, they just end up in landfills or incinerators. The energy needed to make one new aluminium can is the same as the energy needed to recycle 20 cans. In the UK alone, there would be 12 million fewer dustbins to empty each year if all aluminium drink cans were recycled.

## Recycling

In industrialized countries such as the UK and the United States, almost half of the contents of our bins could be recycled. Recycling means transforming waste into usable resources. It can involve turning old material into a new version of the same thing, or into something completely different. For example, glass bottles can be recycled into new bottles, or plastic bottles can be used to make fleeces. However, recycling only works if there is a demand for the recycled products. Many people believe that things made from recycled materials are of lower quality than if they were made from new materials. As a result, in many countries, materials are piling up in recycling plants. Another problem is that materials such as plastics are difficult to recycle and need to be separated at source. For example, milk and washing-up liquid bottles are made of

### RECYCLING

Did you know that:

- The energy saved by recycling one glass bottle will power a computer for 25 minutes, or a television for 20 minutes, or a washing machine for 10 minutes.
- Recycling 7 steel cans saves enough energy to power a light bulb for 26 hours.
- Producing an aluminium can from recycled material can save enough energy to run a television for three hours.

a different kind of plastic from margarine tubs and carrier bags. If they are not separated carefully, the plastic cannot be recycled.

## Composting

A simple way of recycling is composting. Composting is the natural breakdown of organic matter by micro-organisms into a rich material that makes a great natural fertilizer. At least 20 to 50 percent of the waste sent to landfills is made up of tree leaves, grass clippings and kitchen wastes. Bagging these materials for kerbside rubbish collection costs a lot of money and has an impact on the environment. In many countries, organic material is collected separately and taken to municipal composting sites. However, even with a small amount of outside space, you can reduce the amount of waste you put in your bin by separating out your organic waste and using it to make your own compost.

An organic farmer in Wisconsin, United States, holds a handful of red wigglers. This type of earthworm is commonly used in composting to help turn organic waste into rich, fertile soil.

### Recycling is cool

Everyone needs to buy recycled products. Innovative companies are constantly coming up with exciting designs for products made from recycled materials. In 1993, Patagonia, a well-known American outdoor clothing company, was the first to adopt fleece made from recycled plastic into its product line. Since that time, Patagonia has saved about 86 million soda bottles from the rubbish heap. In 2003,

**A giant stack of textiles awaits recycling. Reuse and recycling of textiles is now a major industry, and products made from recycled materials are appearing on the high street and in the fashion industry.**

Sotheby's, the London auction house, promoted waste as a material for creating exciting design through a contemporary art and design exhibition. The exhibition included clothes with gold-sprayed coffee filter bags, mirrors made of decorative scraps of materials and a selection of quirky lamps made of old machine parts. Stylish bags from recycled materials such as plastic, car upholstery, juice box labels and skateboard decks can be bought on the high street. For example, the company Relan transforms old billboards from outdoor advertising companies into handbags. Pencil cases and computer mousepads are made from the rubber from discarded tyres. And in Canada you can buy copies of some of the Harry Potter books that are printed on 100 percent recycled paper.

### On the catwalk

Reusing and recycling textiles is an old idea but it is now a big industry. The clothes we wear and the textiles used to make them can have a huge impact on the environment. For example, the pesticides used by farmers to grow cotton, the chemicals used to colour textiles and the old clothes that we throw away, all contribute to waste. Most of these clothes could be recycled or reused.

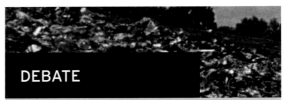

**DEBATE**

**You are in charge**
Think about a day in your life and all the things you do, buy, consume and throw away. Try to identify three actions that would help to reduce waste at home or at school. How would you persuade friends and family to take action?

The good news is that clothes made from recycled materials are now appearing on the catwalk. In Denmark, Earth A'Wear was the first shop to stock only 'green' clothes on the high street. All their clothes are made from environmentally-friendly or recycled materials. For example, skirts are made from pineapple fibres and belts from bicycle tyres. In 1995, the Italian designer label Armani started to recycle old jeans into new ones. Armani has since created a line of clothing made from hemp, a fast-growing plant that is environmentally friendly because it needs no pesticides or herbicides, uses little water and does not deplete the nutrients in the soil. The German adventure sports manufacturer Salewa produces clothes made from maize (sweetcorn) plants. The maize is fermented to produce a substance from which fibres are made. The clothes made from this material are lightweight and breathable, and at the end of their use they can be composted.

# CHAPTER 6

# Time to Change

**It is 2025.** World leaders are gathering in Beijing for a third Earth Summit. The waste crisis has become a global problem and the agenda will focus mainly on action towards sustainable waste. Sixty percent of the countries that submitted a report in preparation for the first Earth Summit in 1992 said that solid waste disposal was one of their biggest environmental concerns. More than 30 years later, most governments have failed to take sufficient action to address the waste crisis. More holes are being dug in the ground to bury rubbish and more incinerators are being built.

Since the last Summit, groups of young people have come together all around the world to initiate real action in their homes, schools and communities. In their view, not enough has been done in the last two decades and they are putting pressure on governments to be given a genuine voice at the Beijing Summit. They are asking governments to adopt a Zero Waste approach to the reduction of waste. They are trying to persuade big companies to introduce the concept of clean production. Young people want to be given a genuine voice at the Summit to present their views, as they are the decision-makers of tomorrow.

**Zoom around the world**

In the 21st century, environmental groups and bodies such as the EU are putting pressure on governments to take real action. In many countries, new programmes are being developed to encourage people to reduce waste and to recycle. Here are a few examples of what happens to waste in different places around the world:

*Switzerland*

In Switzerland, throwing rubbish away costs money. The Swiss have to pay for the number of rubbish bags they fill. About 47 percent of the municipal waste is recycled or composted. Recyclable materials are recovered by retailers and producers. Electronic goods such as computers, TVs and fridges have a recycling tax, and toxic waste has to be disposed of at special sites.

### Denmark

In Denmark, waste is a resource. Waste is taxed if it goes to landfills and incinerators, but is exempt of tax when recycled. Packaging, plastic bags and batteries are taxed in order to reduce e-waste. More than a third of all household waste is recycled. However, the total amount of waste is not big enough for Denmark to have its own recycling plants, so plastic, e-waste, batteries and metal are sent abroad for recycling. The government encourages industry to reduce waste and cleaner technologies are subsidized.

### Germany

In Germany, the polluters have to pay. Different types of materials are collected for recycling. Legally, toxic waste such as batteries or chemicals has to be taken to special recycling centres. Manufacturers have to take back their packaging. Consumers pay a deposit on packaging that can be recycled, such as cans and plastic bottles.

**A German worker sorts electronic waste along a conveyor at a processing centre. In Germany, electronics manufacturers bear the expense of recycling. Electronic equipment, from mobile phones to deep freezers, is collected and sorted at processing centres like this one.**

### Ireland

In Ireland, a tax on plastic shopping bags was introduced in 2002. This has meant that shoppers now buy and reuse their bags, and has led to a reduction of more than 90 percent in the number of plastic bags used by Irish shoppers.

### United States

In the United States, methods of waste disposal and recycling rates vary from state to state. More than 6,000 cities have adopted pay-as-you-throw programmes, in which residents pay for the amount of rubbish they produce. The rate of recycling has almost doubled during the past 15 years. In San Diego county, California, all materials that can be recycled are banned from landfills.

*Senegal*

In Senegal, recycling is not done on an industrial scale, but it is part of daily life. Everything is reused or recycled, from plastic bags to school notebooks, food cans, plastic bottles and organic waste. Tins become drink cups, and old newspapers are used to wrap food. Artisans use metal waste to produce anything from chairs to children's toys.

*China*

China offers tax breaks to companies that recycle waste or use recycled products. China has recently put a tax on disposable chopsticks, sold in billions every year, to reduce waste and the use of timber. Taxes have been raised on luxury items such as yachts, large cars and wooden floor panels.

*Latin America*

Clean power plants operate in Brazil, Argentina, Chile and Venezuela turning biomass (plant and organic matter) into electricity for over five million customers.

## One world

The waste crisis is a global problem that needs a global response. At an international level, countries have come together to agree on clear targets to tackle the problems associated with waste. For example, in 1989, the Basel Convention was created by the world community to control the movement of hazardous waste from one country to another, specifically to prevent rich, industrialized countries from dumping their electronic and toxic waste on poorer countries. The convention, signed by more than 150 nations, came into force in 1992 with the aim of reducing the creation of toxic waste and disposing of it as close to its source as possible. The United States, however, has yet to ratify the agreement despite the fact that it creates a third of global toxic waste.

---

### TACKLING WASTE

**Statements from international agreements relating to waste:**

*'Environmentally sound management of hazardous wastes or other wastes means taking all practicable steps to ensure that [such] ... wastes are managed in a manner which will protect human health and the environment against the adverse effects which may result from such wastes.'*
Basel Convention, 1989

*'Overall objective ... To prevent or minimize the generation of waste. This should be part of an overall cleaner production approach; by 2010, all countries should have national plans for waste management.'*
Agenda 21, chapters 20 and 22

---

In 1997, the Kyoto Protocol set a target for reducing emissions of carbon dioxide and other greenhouse gases by 5 percent by 2012. Although some industrialized countries such as the United States and Australia have not yet agreed to the Protocol, it still marks an important international commitment to reducing emissions that contribute to global warming. These targets, even though they are not always met, are a huge step forward as they indicate a commitment from nations around the world and highlight areas where progress needs to be made.

A cyclist rides past a wall mosaic installed by the environmental pressure group Friends of the Earth outside the United Nations Climate Change Conference in Montreal, in November 2005. The words 'Make Kyoto Live Today!' remind politicians of the targets set in Kyoto to reduce greenhouse gases.

## An agenda for the 21st century

Agenda 21, an action plan for the 21st century, was adopted by 179 nations at the Earth Summit in 1992. It devotes three specific chapters to the problem of waste. Agenda 21 says that we need to reduce waste, recycle, and tax packaging materials. Industry needs to adopt cleaner production methods and new technologies should be made available to less developed countries. It also talks about the importance of informing people about the risks of the chemicals they are exposed to, and the need to clean up contaminated areas and give help to their inhabitants. It supports the idea of making the polluters pay and promotes a ban on the export of toxic waste to countries not equipped to deal with it. Agenda 21 promotes the adoption of sustainable patterns of production and consumption and the need to stop the excessive use of natural resources, such as wood.

## Zero Waste

Zero Waste is a new approach to waste based on the idea that we can eliminate it altogether. As the world's population continues to rise, the system of extracting resources to make packaging and products that will later be burned or buried is not sustainable. Zero Waste is a different way of looking at things. It goes beyond recycling and entails redesigning products and changing the way waste is handled so that products last longer and materials are recycled. Waste is seen as a resource and means jobs for people, money for businesses and industries, and material for new products.

In some industrialized countries such as Canada and Australia, leading corporations, municipalities and governments are coming

Tom Szaky is the co-founder of TerraCycle, a company that produces organic plant food. Organic waste is fed to millions of worms and this natural fertilizer is then liquefied and bottled in used soda bottles. There are collection points for used bottles all across the United States. This is a product entirely 'made from and packaged in waste'.

together to adopt strategies towards a Zero Waste society. The aim is to reduce the amount of toxic waste they produce and to conserve and recover all resources. Zero Waste means no waste goes to landfills and incinerators. It means that producers are responsible for the products and packaging they produce, and that consumers must reuse or buy recycled products. It means that governments must provide financial incentives for consumers and producers to reduce waste.

### Zero Waste in action

An increasing number of cities and states have adopted the goal of Zero Waste, including Canberra in Australia, Toronto in Canada, and the state of California in the United States. In 2002, New Zealand became the first country in the world to adopt this strategy. Through different programmes and incentives, the New Zealand government is working with industry, businesses and communities to increase recycling, reduce waste, reduce consumption and ensure that products are made to be reused, repaired, recycled or composted.

## PLEASE REUSE THIS BOOK!

It takes approximately 17 trees to make one tonne of paper, not to mention large amounts of water, chemicals such as chlorine and sulphur, and energy. So please make sure that when you have finished with this book you pass it on to a friend.

## DEBATE

**You are in charge**
You are a member of a youth delegation representing your country at the Summit on Sustainable Waste. What actions will you take?

- Identify the main problems in your own environment with your friends, family and teachers.
- Suggest an action plan on how you can encourage waste reduction.
- Challenge your leaders to bring the waste issue to the centre of local and national decision-making.

# Glossary

**Agenda 21** An international agreement to reduce the impact of human action on the world's environment.

**asbestos** A mineral made of long fibres, which is resistant to chemicals and non-flammable, and therefore used as a heat-resistant material. Asbestos can damage people's health as the fibres get stuck in their lungs.

**aseptic** Germ-free.

**bauxite** The mineral that is used to make aluminium.

**biodegradable waste** Waste that breaks down or rots naturally when attacked by bacteria. Examples include food and garden waste.

**biomass** Plant material or agricultural waste used as a fuel or energy source.

**cadmium** A metallic element found mainly in zinc, copper and lead ores.

**climate change** The process of long-term changes to the world's climate, increasingly as a result of human activities polluting the atmosphere.

**compost** A mixture of organic household waste (for example, vegetable peelings and brown cardboard) and plants that have decomposed over time.

**consumption** The use of resources, products and services by consumers.

**contaminate** To pollute or expose to radioactivity.

**corrosive** A substance that can eat away or consume materials such as metals by chemical action.

**emissions** Gases released into the atmosphere.

**ferrous metal** Metal that contains iron.

**greenhouse emissions** The atmosphere works like a greenhouse, trapping the sun's heat and warming the earth. Human activity has increased the level of gases such as carbon dioxide and methane in the atmosphere. These 'greenhouse' gases trap more heat, making the earth warmer.

**hazardous** Something that is dangerous to humans, other living things and the environment.

**heavy metals** Metallic elements that can be harmful to living things and which tend to build up in the food chain. Heavy metals include chromium, mercury, cadmium, arsenic and lead.

**incineration** The process of burning combustible waste, producing heat, gases and ash. The heat can be used to generate electricity. However, incineration also releases toxic gases.

**jute** A tropical plant that is grown for its strong fibres.

**landfill** A site where waste materials are deposited into or on the ground.

**leachate** Rainwater that seeps through a landfill and becomes contaminated. If not contained and managed properly, leachate can pollute groundwater, rivers and coastal areas.

**methane** A highly flammable gas released by landfill sites which contributes to global warming.

**micro-organism** An organism of micro-scopic size such as a bacterium.

**municipal solid waste** The solid waste produced by homes, schools, offices and shops.

**natural resources** Substances of use to humans that are derived from the earth (for example, coal, wood, metal ores) or from living things.

**non-governmental organization** (NGO) A non-profit organization that is independent of government.

**nutrient** Any of the minerals that are absorbed by plants or animals as food.

**organic waste** Waste derived from plants and animals.

**pesticide** A chemical used to kill insects and other pests.

**pollutant** Something that contaminates air, soil or water.

**radiation** Energy that is transmitted in the form of rays, waves or particles.

**radioactive** Some elements such as uranium or plutonium are radioactive. This means they give out radiation as they change into other elements.

**raw materials** The basic resources used to make materials and products. For example, bauxite is extracted from the earth to make aluminium.

**recycling** Using materials that have been used before to make new things. Materials that can be recycled include glass, paper, cardboard, steel, aluminium and plastic.

**residue** Matter remaining after something has been removed. For example, residues from incineration include toxic ashes.

**sustainable consumption** Sustainable consumption is about using goods and services that meet our basic needs and bring a better quality of life for all, whilst minimizing the use of natural resources, waste and pollution. It is also about sharing resources between rich and poor and acting with concern for future generations.

**toxic waste** Waste that is poisonous to humans or other living things.

**Zero Waste** A goal that, if met, would result in very little waste being created; instead, people would find ways to reduce the amount of materials used in the first place and to reuse or recycle unwanted materials.

# Further Information

## Books

*21st Century Debates: Waste, Recycling and Reuse* by Rob Bowden (Hodder Wayland, 2003)

*Green Files: Waste and Recycling* by Steve Parker (Heinemann Library, 2003)

*Planet under Pressure: Waste* by Clive Gifford (Raintree, 2005)

*Sustainable Futures: Waste, Recycling and Reuse* by Sally Morgan (Evans Brothers, 2005)

## Websites

www.environment-agency.gov.uk/
A site produced by the UK Environment Agency which provides information on the themes of waste, plastics and the three 'R's – reduce, reuse and recycle. If you live in the UK, you can put in the postcode of your home or school and find out about landfill sites, pollution, and other environmental issues in your local area.

epa.gov/kids/
A site for children produced by the US Environmental Protection Agency, providing facts and action you can take.

www.recyclezone.org.uk/
A UK site produced by Waste Watch for schools, children and teachers providing useful information, facts and data about the problem of waste.

www.treehugger.com/
A web magazine that gives information on recycled products and discusses the impact of waste on the environment.

www.wasteonline.org.uk/
A great source of information on every aspect of waste.

www.weeeman.org/
An initiative to raise awareness of the amount of electrical and electronic equipment the average person in the UK produces. The site allows you to measure your own impact.

www.youthxchange.net/
A website full of information from all around the world about reducing waste and sustainable consumption.

# Debate Panel answers

**Page 11:**
Solutions to the problem of waste are not simple. When we bury or burn our rubbish we are losing valuable resources and energy. Recycling can be costly and impractical. A combination of actions from consumers, businesses, manufacturers and governments is needed. Many people believe that governments need to take direct actions that will force changes. They argue that by taxing wasteful and polluting activities governments are able to influence businesses, industries and individuals to change their attitudes towards waste.

**Page 19:**
When recycling electronic waste, you need to make sure that the waste is not sent abroad and that you deal only with responsible recyclers. To find out about schemes in your local area, you can look at directories on the Internet.

**Page 27:**
When considering the packaging of mobile phones, these questions might be helpful. Is the item over-packaged? Is the package recyclable or made of recyclable material? Is it biodegradable? Can the package be recovered from consumers? And do mobile phones need to be changed every year?

**Page 32:**
To help you with this debate, you could investigate what ends up in a typical household bin over a week. (Please make sure that you wear protective gloves when examining the contents of your bin!) What actions could you take to encourage everybody in your neighbourhood to reduce, reuse and recycle their waste? For example, you could set up a task force in your local area with representatives from government, local businesses and the community. What actions could you take to encourage the government to tackle the crisis? For example, you could suggest ideas for making recycling easier, or making manufacturers responsible for the waste they produce. What actions could you take to target industry and the business sector? For example, you could write letters to ask companies to stop sending junk mail that you don't want, or to reduce the amount of food packaging that ends up in your bin.

**Page 39:**
Here are a few tips to reduce waste. Buy only the amount you need. Give preference to objects that can be recycled, repaired or are reusable. Avoid disposable products such as plastic cups, cameras and batteries that contribute to landfill problems. Avoid items that are over-packaged. Take your own bags to do your shopping to avoid using plastic bags. Recycle materials such as cans, plastic, card, paper and glass and compost food and garden waste.

**Page 45:**
It will take more than recycling a few cans to sort out the problem of waste. You can participate in decisions that affect you. Make your voice heard. Find out what are the main issues related to waste where you live. Identify practical actions that you can take. For example, you could write to companies to tell them that you will not buy their products unless they reduce their packaging or use recyclable materials. You could contact your local authority to find out why some kinds of materials are not recycled.

# Index

Page numbers in **bold** refer to illustrations.